Are we n there yet?

Jenny Hawke

Dedication

For my beautiful nieces Claudia and Georgia,
whose energy, laughter and love of life enriches
mine. And for Judith, my editor, who gave me
the chance to write. I will always be grateful.

Are we nearly there yet?
by
Jenny Hawke

Other books by Jenny Hawke
Elephants in the Rush Hour

Other books by Eddie Askew and Jenny Hawke
Walking into the Light
Making a Mark
There was a Garden

Published, edited and distributed by TLM Trading Limited
www.tlmtrading.com

First Published 2013
Text and Paintings © Jenny Hawke

Jenny Hawke has asserted her right to be identified as the author of this work in accordance with the Copyright, Designs and Patents Act, 1988.

All rights and subsidiary rights have been granted to
The Leprosy Mission Trading Limited.

Design and production by Creative Plus Publishing Ltd,
www.creative-plus.co.uk

Printed and bound in Singapore by Imago

ISBN 978-1-909092-09-9

Foreword

Thinking back over my childhood, which for me happened to be in India, I remember plenty of long journeys. Some over dusty and difficult roads in the back of a jeep that had little or no suspension, and others by train and a small plane to boarding school in Darjeeling in the Himalayas. Some were exciting and filled with tension, others were just too long and boring for a small and impatient child. The best journeys were always those that brought me home.

'Are we nearly there yet?' echoes the predictable cry of impatient children everywhere, but it also touches on our continuing journey as adults. Some of our days will be full of laughter and fun, while others will be more serious as we have to travel on difficult and perhaps unplanned roads. I hope this book will bring you a sense of sun and shade, colour and direction for the day ahead of you. Our life journey continues as we grow older, and I, for one, am very thankful that we have a God who travels with us.

This is what the Lord says: "Stand at the crossroads and look; ask for the ancient paths, ask where the good way is, and walk in it, and you will find rest for your souls."
Jeremiah 6:16 (New International Version)

Blessings,

Jenny Hawke

Are we nearly there yet?

Romans 15:5
God is the one who makes us patient and cheerful.
(*Contemporary English Version*)

As a child in India I used to love to travel with Mum and Dad in the old Land Rover to Calcutta, now Kolkata. Dad would sometimes have meetings there so we would all pile in with our luggage and drive out of the compound and off down the Grand Trunk Road. The roads in those days were more dirt roads than tarmac, with potholes around every bend and so the journey could take many hours though that wasn't really the problem. The problem was me. Within a few minutes I would be asking the inevitable question, 'Are we nearly there yet?'

I think it's a question every parent dreads on a long journey, especially after only ten minutes of driving. The restless child with little concept of time and a low boredom threshold is a potential nightmare.

My problem was, and still is, that I am impatient. When I decide to go somewhere I am there in my mind already and so I find myself rushing through life, trying to get 'there' as soon as possible. When I stop and think about it, I am often not sure why I am rushing and what good it will do me to get there a few minutes early. It is a tiring way to live.

It seems a shame to rush and miss the beauty of the journey. In India the Grand Trunk Road would pass through some beautiful countryside. We'd see enormous banyan trees with massive roots spreading into the ground, giving shade for herds of goats and a roaming cow or two. We'd pass through villages with colourful food stalls, and often children would run after our jeep shouting and laughing. There were always long convoys of lorries travelling on the same road, completely painted in vibrant colours and decorated with flags. So much to enjoy.

Maybe because I am getting older I am learning to slow down a little and enjoy the process rather than just the end result. I would love to be back on the road in India right now, potholes and all. Worcester Park High Street isn't quite the same, but it is where I live and it's where I am happy. Who knows what is to come in the future, but I'm going to make sure I make the most of it along the way.

Lord, I'm rushing again,
thinking of the day ahead
and all I want to do.
The list is long,
but it's of my making.
Let me pause, Lord,
and simply breathe in your goodness,
and put my list aside,
just for a moment.
Be my still point, Lord,
the peace at my centre,
as I begin this day
with you.

Games with a seal

Isaiah 11:6
And the wolf shall dwell with the lamb, and the leopard shall lie down with the kid;
and the calf and the young lion and the fatted domestic animal together;
and a little child shall lead them.

(*American Standard Version*)

On a small beach in St Ives, surrounded by dogs and their owners, we were watching Mortimer playing. Actually, what he was doing was waiting for the right moment to steal the ball from another dog and run away with it, forcing the other dogs to chase him and so giving him the opportunity to join their game. Morty is our big, fluffy, white Labradoodle who is often mistaken for a sheep. We've lost count of the times when someone has said, 'Is that a dog?' Anyway, Morty had joyfully and successfully muscled in on the game, and soon, a red ball was being thrown into the sea followed by numerous dogs splashing frantically towards it.

And then we saw something amazing. A large seal was approaching the shore close to the swimming dogs. We held our breath as we saw it swim closer and closer. Seals are sometimes reported to be quite aggressive to dogs, but the ball was still in the water and a big brown dog was swimming out to it. The seal got there first and nosed the ball up out of the water, then the dog grabbed the ball and swam for the shore. We couldn't believe what we were seeing as the seal followed the dog within an inch of its tail, looking as if it was keen to play. The seal turned away when it hit the shallows and then seemed to wait.

The ball was thrown again and again, and we saw the same thing happen. Each time the seal would toss the ball and then follow the dog in towards the shore. A small crowd had gathered on the stone steps and on the sea wall, all watching this remarkable moment when a wild animal was interacting peacefully with a tame one. Looking back now, I realise the seal had been close enough to attack at any time but chose not to. It really seemed to be playing.

I've been wondering why this event made such an impact on me and I've come to the conclusion that I can hear echoes of the story of Eden, and the promise of the life to come. The Bible says that there will be a new heaven and a new earth, and in Isaiah 11:6 it talks of the wild animals lying down with domestic ones and a little child being with them and not coming to harm.

We see our world and know that it is not as it should be, and so, when we experience times like this, I think our hearts leap because we see a glimpse of the new life that is promised. It was a remarkable occasion and I am so grateful that I was there to witness this foretaste of heaven.

Lord,
I know things are not
as they should be,
both in my own life,
and in the world around me.
But thank you for such a glimpse
of how things once were
and how they will be again.
A seal and a dog,
at play with a ball.
A remarkable thing.
It gives me hope,
and a window into
the joy that's to come.
A simple illustration
of the absence of fear
and the presence of
a greater trust.
Thank you.

A work in progress

2 Corinthians 3:18
So all of us who have had that veil removed can see and reflect the glory
of the Lord. And the Lord – who is the Spirit – makes us more and more
like him as we are changed into his glorious image.
(*New Living Translation*)

I met an amazing artist the other day. I was attending a workshop with a
tutor called Marion Taylor. She encouraged us to experiment and to interpret
what we see in a different way. Later in the day, I went to her studio. On the
wall was one very large picture, which was probably as tall as me. She had

begun the painting months ago, using dark colours in order to depict Hong Kong harbour.

The picture had already been shown in a gallery, but when it was returned, she looked at it again and felt strongly that it still wasn't finished. She kept looking at the painting, until one day she decided to add some more paint by literally throwing it onto the canvas. She chose bright orange, in stark contrast to the greys, blues and blacks, but it looked wonderful. She felt that it was finally finished.

I don't know how any artist knows when their own painting is finished, but they just do. Marion explained the splash of orange was her comment on the pollution of the harbour against the beauty that remained. This story reminds me that I am also a work in progress and that God is not finished with me yet. We are told that we are continually being transformed. In fact, I heard someone put it like this...

'I am not as I was and I am not as I shall be, for I am being continually changed from glory to glory.'

I like that. On my bad days, it gives me hope that God who made me is still working on me. He sees the full picture and like the artist, he will know when his work in me is completed!

Lord, I love painting,
often never knowing how it will
look in the end.
Adding colours,
dropping water from the brush.
Standing back,
watching how they mix,
taking shape,
finding beauty on the page.
Is my life like that, Lord?
Sometimes I can see the beauty in it.
Though it's easier to see that
in someone else's life.
I often see the mess in my own life,
even when I'm searching for sense
and looking for purpose.

But if I stand back,
in your presence,
and take another look,
there is beauty in my history,
and I can see your hand,
The unmistakable signs,
that you are still working in me,
and through me,
and that you're not finished yet.
Until then, Lord,
I will wait and watch
for more of the beauty to emerge.

Jesus is in the house

Mark 2:1–2
And Jesus having returned to Capernaum, after some days it was rumoured about that He was in the house [probably Peter's]. And so many people gathered together there that there was no longer room [for them], not even around the door; and He was discussing the Word.
(*Amplified Bible*)

There is a phrase in a familiar story that has grabbed my attention. It is the story of Jesus going to Peter's house. I have read the story many times, and seen it in my mind. The excited crowds, the heat and dust, the darkness inside as people rush in. Recently, my imagination took off when someone pointed to the phrase 'it was rumoured about that He was in the house.'

Can you imagine it! Jesus is in a house in the next town, the next village, the next city. I would drop everything, ring my friends, send texts, put messages on Facebook, e-mail everyone and spread the word as I ran towards the village, heart beating and not really able to believe I was actually going to see Him.

We don't live in those times anymore, but there are some times when the presence of God is so strong, so tangible and so real that it takes your breath away. And if you hear that something special like this is going on near where you live, go and see and experience it for yourself.

I've been reading about the Welsh revival (the Christian revival in Wales in the early 20th century) recently, and it reminds me of the excitement of those times. It is said that people came from miles around just to get into one of the meetings where revival was happening. And so would I. The football stadiums were empty, as were the pubs, and the crime rate dropped to an all-time low as everywhere people were chasing the presence of God. In fact, people were walking the streets singing and praying at all times of the day and night.

I long for another revival like that in this country, and some say that it is indeed coming. All I know is that I will keep listening and keep hoping to hear that 'Jesus is in town' and then I'll tell everyone I know and set off running...

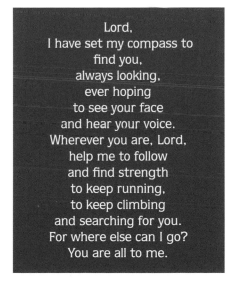

Lord,
I have set my compass to
find you,
always looking,
ever hoping
to see your face
and hear your voice.
Wherever you are, Lord,
help me to follow
and find strength
to keep running,
to keep climbing
and searching for you.
For where else can I go?
You are all to me.

We are beloved

Song of Solomon 7:10

I belong to my beloved, and his desire is for me.

(*New International Version*)

My lovely daughter has the ability to find the most beautiful poems, she sometimes passes them on to me. Her timing is often perfect. She showed me a beautiful poem about life, during the Christmas holidays, a time when expectations are high, and family stress levels can be at a similar level.

In this particular poem, the poet, Raymond Carver, asks a question about what we want in life, And the answer he receives is one we can all identify with…

"To call myself beloved, to feel myself beloved on the earth."
(from 'Late Fragment', by Raymond Carver, 1938–88.)

Christmas and New Year are times when we look back over the year and I'm tempted to get drawn in to thinking of all the things I have or haven't done in a negative way. These beautiful words drew me back to the bigger picture. To know that I am loved, in fact beloved, and to feel it. To know in the depths of my being that in spite of all that I think of myself and my failings, I am blessed by having good friends and family and I am loved deeply by my God. It is a miracle and it helps me to see myself in a different and more kindly light. We are loved and even though it might take us a lifetime to accept it fully, it doesn't change this wonderful truth.

Through Jesus, we are beloved, and we are blessed.

> Lord, I do not understand
> your love for me,
> but I know it continues
> day after day,
> regardless of my circumstance
> or my ever-shifting feelings.
> I am loved to a depth I cannot
> fully imagine.
> Words are a poor reflection
> to describe my response,
> except to say, "Thank you."
> And Lord, let me be part
> of showing others
> that they too are beloved
> on this earth.

Plain English

John 16:25

Though I have been speaking figuratively, a time is coming when I will no longer use this kind of language but will tell you plainly about my Father.

(New International Version)

I was at a conference last week where each day started with a prayer. It began well enough, committing the day to the Lord, but somewhere along the line, the language seemed to change, and the prayer was suddenly full of clichés that only people 'in the know' would understand. In my mind, I could hear Dad saying quietly, 'And now let's have the English version.'

I am not criticising the prayer, just the language. It is too easy to use phrases that cannot be understood by non-Christians. And then it feels a little exclusive. Phrases that I dislike particularly are... 'The Lord has put it on my heart' and 'We've been washed in the blood of the Lamb'. There is nothing wrong with the meaning of them, unless taken literally, but they are so hard for people who are not familiar with the church to understand.

I've had similar experiences visiting some galleries. The descriptions of the paintings are written in 'art-speak', not easily understood by you or me, talking about concepts that I don't understand because I haven't read the right book. We can be left with a rather unhelpful 'us and them' feeling.

Jesus spoke in everyday language, using stories from the world around him. He used pictures of everyday life, tales of fishermen and their catch, shepherds and sheep. Our speech needs to be relevant to the world around us, clearly pointing the way to Jesus, so people don't get lost listening to what can feel like a foreign language. The message of the Gospel is simple. Let's keep our language simple and accessible too.

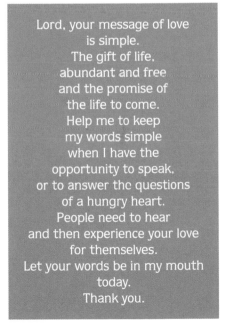

Lord, your message of love
is simple.
The gift of life,
abundant and free
and the promise of
the life to come.
Help me to keep
my words simple
when I have the
opportunity to speak,
or to answer the questions
of a hungry heart.
People need to hear
and then experience your love
for themselves.
Let your words be in my mouth
today.
Thank you.

In the shadow

Acts 5:15

...people brought those who were ill into the streets and laid them on beds and mats so that at least Peter's shadow might fall on some of them as he passed by.
(*New International Version*)

I was watching *The Best Exotic Marigold Hotel* last night for the third time. If you haven't seen it yet, please do, as I think you'll enjoy it. It's a gently uplifting film with some beautiful snapshots of India, even though it is a little stereotypical in parts.

One particular line grabbed my attention. Maggie Smith, who plays a wonderfully cantankerous woman fallen on hard times, is trying to speak to the young woman who brings her food every day. Another guest intervenes, explaining that she won't understand English because she is one of the Dalits, formerly known as 'the untouchables'. A true Hindu believes that if a Dalit's shadow falls on you, you will be polluted, hence they will avoid any contact with them at all costs.

My mind suddenly jumped back two thousand years to the mention of someone else's shadow. In *The Message*, a wonderful modern translation of the Bible, it says, 'They even carried the sick out into the streets and laid them on stretchers and bedrolls, hoping they would be touched by Peter's shadow when he walked by. They came from the villages surrounding Jerusalem, throngs of them, bringing the sick and bedeviled. And they all were healed.'

What a contrast. The shadow of a young woman, shunned by society, working

Lord,
it's just a shadow,
a simple outline of someone
in the sun.
Innocent of meaning,
unless we give it one.
Peter Pan ran from his shadow,
children make shapes and
laugh at theirs,
yet others fear contamination
giving what is natural
a power it should not have.

Lord, you came to redeem
what has been lost,
to free us from
crippling prejudice
and bring life in abundance.
Lord, would you do that
through me?
Let me be part of the
transformation,
where darkness is brought
into light
and justice is mixed freely
with love.
And all this can only happen
through you.
Lord, let it be,
and I'll stand with you.

hard to support her family, mistakenly thought to have the power to pollute, while the shadow of a follower of Jesus is seen by witnesses to carry the power to heal.

I was reminded of a visit to Kolkata, India, a few years ago. Our guide had brought us to see Mother Teresa's Home for the Destitute and Dying. Outside the home, we met a group of lively young children who were eager to say hello to us. We responded by talking and laughing with them and holding hands with some of them. I remember looking up and seeing the expression on our guide's face. It was one of intense disapproval. "Madam," he said, "you should be careful what you touch. You might pick up some disease." These lovely children were from the Dalit community – we simply saw them as children.

This is the redeeming beauty of the gospel, freedom from slavery, prejudice and injustice, and the hope of healing. And that's how our society should be. Thankfully, there are people working on behalf of the Dalit community trying to break the hold of such damaging beliefs. Let's pray that we can challenge prejudice wherever we meet it, and bring the freedom and love of God in its place.

And the towel got dirty

John 13:2–5

The evening meal was in progress… Jesus knew that the Father had put all things under his power, and that he had come from God and was returning to God; so he got up from the meal, took off his outer clothing and wrapped a towel around his waist. After that, he poured water into a basin and began to wash his disciples' feet, drying them with the towel wrapped round him.

(New International Version)

I've never had my feet washed, by someone else that is, and especially not in public, but the disciples did. We know the story well. It was Passover. Jesus knew what was about to happen to him and he had gathered the disciples together for the Passover meal. Then he stood up and, having wrapped a towel around him, began what must have been unthinkable in the disciples' minds, he began to wash their feet. The rabbi, the teacher, on his knees washing twelve pairs of incredibly dirty feet.

Lord,
what an amazing scene.
You, the King of Kings,
on your knees
gently washing twelve
pairs of feet,
making them clean.
Water splashing onto the floor
and the muddy towel
in your hands.
A small act
with eternal impact.

Thank you for showing the way,
for getting on your knees
for me.
As Peter said,
'Don't just wash my feet,
but my hands and my head
as well.
And lead me on
to do the same for others.

And have you ever thought how dirty the towel must have been? It might seem a very strange question, but it seems to me that we can easily have a very sanitized picture of Jesus no matter where we imagine him and what we imagine him doing. I'm not sure why I was suddenly struck by this thought, or why it matters, except perhaps because the reality of helping people can be messy and difficult. The disciples were embarrassed, not only because their feet must have been very dusty and dirty, but also because they realised they should have washed Jesus' feet first. Hospitality, love, kindness, call it what you will, but the Lord didn't hesitate. He took off his outer garment and began acting out for real the lesson he wanted them to learn.

I like things to be easy and under my control. I want to help people of course, but when things get messy, my resolve

can waver. Jesus didn't hesitate. He didn't wait for someone else to get started, he stepped in straight away. The towel got dirty and the disciples learnt a lesson they would never forget. And neither should we.

Let's get volunteering, we might need to get our hands dirty, we might need to get involved in a messy situation, but let's show people we care. Cook a meal for someone, volunteer at a rest home, clear someone's overgrown garden, start a charity, go on a sponsored walk, fight for a cause, organise a petition. There are hundreds of opportunities out there. We simply need to get started.

Let's bin the cakes!

Isaiah 61:3
...he will give a crown of beauty for ashes,
a joyous blessing instead of mourning,
festive praise instead of despair...
(*New Living Translation*)

The mother of an old school friend of mine died recently and I was invited to her funeral. After the service we went back to the house for a light lunch. I was helping in the kitchen amongst the growing mountains of sandwiches, when my friend came in carrying an open box of cakes.

She looked rather shocked and began to explain… The bakery had rung her that morning to say they had run out of the pastries she had ordered, so Lorraine simply asked them to substitute the order with something similar. When she opened the box she saw what looked like edible coffins with a dark streak of jam down the middle and a rice paper skull at one end of every cake.

They were indeed meant to be coffins as these were Hallowe'en cakes. The funeral was only a few days before Hallowe'en. Hardly appropriate, but they hadn't realised that the order was for a funeral gathering. My friend looked shocked for a few seconds and then began to laugh, and thankfully, the laughter spread. She realised that her mum would have been the very first to see the funny side of the situation. We decided that even after the rice paper skulls were removed, the cakes still looked like coffins and, as none of us like Hallowe'en, the cakes were thrown away.

The situation could have gone one of two ways, my friend could have burst into tears and accused the bakery of ruining her mother's funeral, but God has given her a great sense of humour and she chose the laughter route.

Sometimes we need to 'accentuate the positive and eliminate the negative' as the song goes. God has gifted us all with a sense of humour and sometimes we need to choose to use it. I'm so glad that funny things can happen even in the midst of sadness; we saw a little of that at the wake. It lifted my friend and her family and reminded them of other happy memories of their mum who also knew the joy of laughter.

Lord,
bless my friend,
and all those who
mourn today.
Walk with them
through shade and light,
and teach them to be
kind to themselves,
to soften their own
expectations of
how to behave,
and how to grieve.
Let them see the joy
though momentary now,
you have promised
more to come.
And thank you for the
gift of humour
that can break into our lives
just when we need it.

Mummy will save me

Isaiah 12:2
I trust you to save me, Lord God, and I won't be afraid.
(Contemporary English Version)

I have a young friend called Grace. She is just six years old and she often comes over for tea. I love talking with her as she sees the world in a refreshingly different way to me. On this particular day, we were chatting when the subject of swimming came up, as she was going to the pool the next day. I asked her if she could swim. When she said, "No!" I asked if she wore a rubber ring or a buoyancy vest. She shook her head vigorously and said, "No, I just jump in." When I showed a little concern at the idea of her sinking under the water, she said, "Ooh yes, but don't worry, Mummy always saves me."

Later, I discovered that swimming was not at all relaxing for Grace's mum, because as soon as Grace was changed and ready, Grace would make a mad dash for the edge of the pool and throw herself in, followed closely by her mum trying frantically to keep up with her.

Grace never does come to any harm because her mummy does always save her, and hopefully she will learn to swim soon. It occurred to me that this is a wonderful picture of faith and trust. Grace has absolutely no doubt that all will be well, as her mummy is always there for her.

We are told that we need to be like children in order to see the Kingdom of God, we need to have a childlike trust in him believing that he will be with us at all times, and will catch us when we fall.

> Such faith, Lord.
> It puts me to shame.
> Like the centurion in the Bible
> who came and asked you
> to heal his servant,
> there was no doubt in his mind.
> He knew your power
> and trusted you to respond.
> Just like Grace.
> To know deep down
> that whatever happens
> all will be well, and all will be well
> and all manner of things
> will be well.
> Let me jump, Lord,
> believing that you will catch
> and hold me.

I protest

Isaiah 1:17
Learn to do right; seek justice. Defend the oppressed.
Take up the cause of the fatherless; plead the case of the widow.
(*New International Version*)

I have been on my first protest, first that is unless you count the March for Jesus inspired by Graham Kendrick in the early seventies as a real protest march! I am in my middle age and just a little embarrassed that it has taken me this long to actively protest or march about anything.

Anyway, I have finally stood up to be counted and it's all because of Sam. Living with our son over the years has been challenging to say the least. He is a young man with very strong principles and an even stronger sense of how the world should be. He alerts us to political crises all over the world, especially at the breakfast table when I am not at my best. Recently, he highlighted the appalling safety and human rights records of a particular mining firm operating all over the world. To cut a long story short, there seemed ample evidence to support what he was saying so we decided to join the protest that day.

Apart from the fact that we met a group of amazing people who are giving all their time and energy to speak out for those who have no voice, we saw first-hand that protesting can and often does make a difference. When the protest was over, we saw on the news that the share price of this particular company had dropped, seemingly as a direct result of the protest and the negative publicity for the firm following it, and that they were indeed closing down some of their unsafe projects.

Lord, it's scary standing up
in public,
making a noise,
joining a protest,
but you did
when you saw injustice
and hypocrisy.
You upset people,
ruffled their tidy feathers,
shook their beliefs
to make them think,
to challenge their behaviour.
Give me courage, Lord.
Help me to find my voice,
to speak up when I feel that nudge
that I know is you.
But more than that,
help me to do it out of love,
and a deep commitment
to people around me,
and Lord, give me the
perseverance
to keep going.

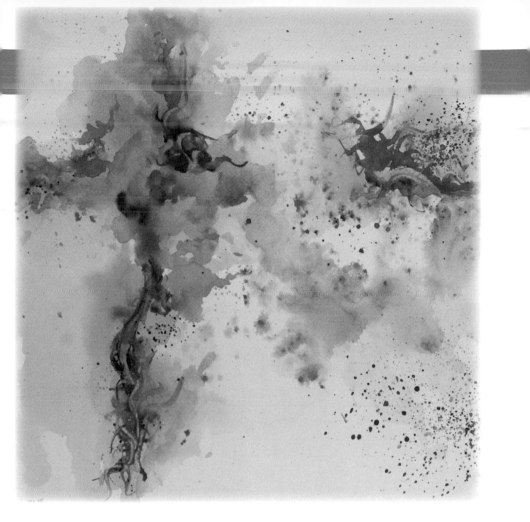

What struck me more were my feelings about being part of that day. Standing up publicly for something you believe in, waving banners, being photographed by the press, and even being slightly intimidated by the police presence was a very new experience. I hate to use the word 'empowered', but I did feel it. We plan to protest about other things that we feel are unjust, so I feel I have found my voice and I think God likes that. He loves justice and He says we should stand up for the poor and oppressed. I can choose to turn away when I see situations that are unfair where 'truth has fallen in the street' (Isaiah 59:14) or I can stop what I am doing, and get involved. Maybe it's time for us all to stick our heads up over the parapet and start shouting until things change. Whether you decide to go on a protest or not, the important thing is to speak out and speak up for those who can't. Let justice rule and reign with love.

Jam first, or clotted cream?

Nehemiah 8:10

Nehemiah said, "Go and enjoy choice food and sweet drinks, and send some to those who have nothing prepared. This day is holy to our Lord..."

(*New International Version*)

Jam first or clotted cream? This may not seem an important question in the scheme of things, but I love cream teas and my husband and I were having an argument about this very issue. We were in the wonderful cafe at the Victoria and Albert museum in London. It looks quite an ordinary cafe when you first go in, but if you turn into one of the rooms on the left, you find yourself in the most amazing Victorian domed room with wall to wall Art Nouveau tiles, stained-glass windows, and a massive chandelier. A great place to enjoy a cream tea and sit and talk. And they even stock my favourite Darjeeling tea. What more could you want?

So there we were, and that's when the argument started.

I always put the jam on my scone first, then the cream as it seems to sit better that way. Peter is of the opposite opinion and so we argued the ins and outs of the situation. Then, I realised that far from enjoying the moment and savouring the jam and cream, however they were put together, we were actually missing out on the moment altogether.

Our argument was put to one side and we concentrated on enjoying our delicious cream tea. However, please feel free to mail my lovely husband your thoughts on this subject, especially if you agree with me, but even better, go to the V&A and try their scones for yourself, if you can. The point being that I feel we need to give ourselves more time to just sit and enjoy the simple pleasures like this.

Lord, sometimes there is nothing nicer -
Darjeeling tea, homemade jam, fresh scones and lashings of cream.
Just once in a while, to simply enjoy the good things in life.
It's too easy to argue the rights and wrongs, the best way to do something, and then the moment has gone.
Teach me to savour these times, to put my lists aside and let myself relax.
Just for a while.

And Lord, will you teach me to rest in your grace today?
Thank you.

A friend said the other day, "If we get this job done, we'll then deserve a rest". We can get into the mindset of feeling that we only deserve to enjoy something if we have really worked hard beforehand. There is some truth in this, but I need to make the most out of any treat I have today whether I deserve it or not. At times it is good to give ourselves a treat, when it is appropriate, and then sit back, relax and enjoy. And that reminds me of the whole idea of God's grace. An undeserved gift. I can never work hard enough to deserve it, but I can learn to fully appreciate and enjoy it.

Whistling for squirrels

Matthew 10:29
Are not two sparrows sold for a penny? Yet not one of them will fall to the ground outside your Father's care.
(*New International Version*)

I was at a conference in London the other day and because I had arrived early I decided to enjoy a walk in nearby Regent's Park. I noticed that a young man walking ahead of me was whistling as if calling a dog. While he kept repeating the call, I was amazed to see several squirrels running towards

him from different directions across the grass. As they approached him, they stopped and waited. He put one leg slightly forwards and continued calling as he held his hand out. One at a time, the squirrels took their turn to scramble up his leg and take a nut from his hand. Each one would then turn, run down his leg and run off to eat it. Then the process would start again.

I decided to follow the man and talk to him. He told me he fed the squirrels like this every day and then offered me some nuts in case I wanted to try doing it myself. I changed direction and began calling just as he had. I held my breath as three squirrels ran towards me. I put one leg forward and waited. One by one, each squirrel ran up to my knee and waited there, clinging to my jeans until I had given them a nut. Amazing. They showed no fear at all as they recognised the call.

> Lord, I need to hear your voice,
> and not just hear it,
> but recognise that it's you,
> calling to me,
> giving direction.
> Like the squirrels
> who knew no fear,
> and came running,
> help me to keep listening for you.
> Keep me close,
> for I know you will provide
> all I need.

Now you may not like squirrels, but, putting that aside, it was a wonderful moment and caused a stir with some of the tourists who were watching. I had to admit to them that this was the first time I had tried it, and pointed in the direction of the man ahead who had shown me how. I like to think there are some Japanese tourists proudly showing their friends back home the photos of the female squirrel whisperer in Regent's Park.

You may, or may not, share my love of animals, but what I realised was that the squirrels responded because they recognised the sound. They had heard it before, knew what it meant, and so they ran to me.

I would like to think I recognise the voice of God in my life as easily as the squirrels recognised their call, and that when I hear His voice I'll change my direction and run towards Him. It's a simple picture, isn't it? A great illustration of how we might try to live our lives. I know I don't always hear clearly, but I guess if I stay close I will hear Him more often.

My remarkable friends

Ephesians 6:13
Therefore put on the full armour of God, so that when the day of evil comes, you may be able to stand your ground, and after you have done everything, to stand.
(New International Version)

I have two quite remarkable friends. I won't name them as I think it would embarrass them deeply, but I have known both of them for some years and have watched them live through serious health issues that have meant they often have high levels of pain on a daily basis. What continues to amaze me is that neither of my friends has become bitter about how life has treated them. And if you heard their stories you would agree with me that they have plenty of reason to be both angry and bitter. They have not only lived with pain but also with the hurt of being badly treated by employers and medical professionals. One friend has even been rejected by her family.

The miracle is that my friends get up to face each day with an amazing interest in the world around them and a loving interest in the life of their friends. I value them both greatly and they inspire me to try to be a better person. In a way, their stories remind me of the long list of difficult experiences Paul and his disciples went through in 2 Corinthians 4:8–9, 'We are hard pressed on every side, but not crushed; perplexed, but not in despair; persecuted, but not abandoned; struck down, but not destroyed…'

> Lord, I know I can stumble
> at the first hurdle,
> but my friends have learnt
> to take the obstacles in
> their stride.
> Their pace may be slow but it
> is steady and I recognise
> your face in them,
> giving them hope
> and the strength to go on.
> Thank you for them for
> I can see their faith in you.
> Lord, bless them today,
> and in the days to come.

When they read this, my friends will feel that I am over-dramatizing their stories, but I believe that the ability to hold on to your own integrity and the sense of who you are through the relentlessness of life is a wonderful thing, and they have both achieved this. In spite of all that has happened, they are still who they are, a joy to be with and wonderful friends to have.

They show a skill I don't always have, an ability to let things go, to move on and not to dwell on things we can't change, the ability to welcome the future without fear. I can see God in both of them, in their patience and in their determination to be themselves and hold on to hope in spite of their outward circumstances. I thank God for their example.

Exchanging a cat for two dogs

Romans 12:2
Do not conform to the pattern of this world, but be transformed by the renewing of your mind. Then you will be able to test and approve what God's will is – his good, pleasing and perfect will.

(*New International Version*)

I was walking in the park the other day with Morty and my son, Sam. We are always on the lookout for any dogs that are brave enough to play with Morty. If you know anything about Labradoodles, you'll know that they have a particular way of playing that can be rather over-enthusiastic. Smaller dogs can often come off worst.

Before long, we met a man with two very small but game dogs who were happy to play. We asked the usual questions asked by all dog owners… How old? What breed? And so on… This turned out to be a more interesting story than usual, simply because the man had agreed with his wife to go to a rescue centre to choose a cat, some while later he returned home with two

dogs instead! I don't remember how he described his wife's initial reaction, but I was really taken with his story!

It occurs to me that we all start out with set ideas of what we want and we make decisions about how our lives should unfold within fixed boundaries. Happily, some of us are more flexible than others in our expectations and the decisions that we make. This lovely man went out for a cat but saw two dogs that desperately needed rehoming together and changed his mind. All worked out well, neither he nor his wife regrets their decision and the dogs are wonderfully happy.

This story made me smile not only because it struck me as funny, but also because it illustrates a different way of living. It features people doing something out of the ordinary, people who are open-minded and ready to respond to something inside that changes one decision for a better one.

I really hope that I can stay flexible, so that I can also be open to new possibilities in my life today.

Keep me flexible Lord, not just
in body but in my mind as well.
I don't want to grow rigid as I age,
carrying fixed opinions that stop me
experiencing new things.

Keep me flexible, Lord and open
my eyes to new possibilities,

new ways of thinking
and even new ways of living,
so I can change my mind,
take a risk,
and embrace what life can
bring today.

The bicycle and the chocolate

Hebrews 12:1
And let us run with perseverance the race marked out for us...
(New International Version)

When I was about six years old, I learnt how to ride a bike. I had a very special 'Aunty', a missionary called Joan Evans, who worked alongside Mum and Dad in India for some years. She had a soft spot for me and one day agreed to help me to learn to ride a bike. But there was a catch. I had to learn in one day, and if I did, she would buy me a bar of chocolate.

Now, for those of you that don't know me, I am a bit of a chocoholic and I don't remember having chocolate that often in India. In fact, I used to dream of heaven being full of chocolate and chewing gum, as both seemed hard to find where we lived in Purulia.

Anyway, the day arrived, and Aunty Joan brought a bike over. This was in the days before small bikes and helpful stabilizers, and I remember my legs being too short for me to sit on the seat. There was a gentle grassy slope to the side of the bungalow and she positioned the bike at the top and I got on. I'm not sure how many times I wobbled down the slope before I managed to keep my balance. It felt like all day, but I had this picture of a bar of chocolate fixed in my mind, so I persevered in my race against the clock to master the bike in one day.

I did learn to ride and I managed it within the deadline, so Aunty Joan brought me my reward though interestingly the memory of learning to ride is stronger than the memory of eating the chocolate. I think the process was more fun.

Lord, would you spur me on,
run with me on the flat,
and help me jump the hurdles?
I need to follow your pace
and keep in step with you,
so I don't get breathless
at the first sign of trouble.
This race we run together
has been set by you
and I need to get into my stride.
I hear you urging me on towards
the finishing line,
ready to welcome me home.
Teach me to enjoy
the full race with you,
and not wish it over too soon,
enjoying the scenery,
the wind on my face,
and the horizon stretching away
in front of me.
Run with me Lord
for I can only do it with you.

That particular 'race' only took one day. Paul talks of our life as a race, urging us on to persevere, to never give up, to follow the example of Jesus. The verse continues, 'for the joy that was set before him he endured the cross.' Life isn't all about bikes and chocolate, and running our own particular race can be hard, but Jesus urges us on. He knows we can persevere with His help, and He will be there at the finishing line to cheer us on.

The blanket

Psalm 139:14 –15

I praise you because I am fearfully and wonderfully made;
your works are wonderful,
I know that full well.
My frame was not hidden from you when
I was made in the secret place,
when I was woven together in the depths of the earth.

(New International Version)

Mum used to do a lot of knitting. She loved complex patterns like Fair Isle and the Kaffe Fasset designs. If she had any wool left over, she would keep it and then knit a square from it. In time, she made a blanket out of the many squares which I now own and have on my bed. Some of the squares are plain but most are patterned with different coloured wools. I love looking at it and can recognise wool from some of the many things she knitted for me and the children.

Last week, at the bottom of her old knitting bag, I found an unfinished square of blue wool that she had been working on before she died. I thought I would finish it for her and then start another row of squares of my own to add to one side of her blanket. Finishing her square didn't take long, maybe half an hour. Once I had cast off, I looked at it again. There was a strange line dividing her stitches from mine, but when I thought about it, the reason was obvious. Her tension was subtly different from mine. We both produced neat stitches, but it was obvious that a different hand had knitted the final few inches.

A poignant moment for me. Holding the square in my hand, I imagined the steady and quick movement of her needles knitting the wool together. Years later, the wool and the needles were the same, but the hands were not. I finished the job for her, but the resulting square told the tale.

I shall still use the square as it reminds me that we are all unique, wonderfully made by God, knitted together in our own mother's womb. Even with the same tools in our hands, and the same pattern, we still leave our own individual mark on life. I can't replicate what my mum did, so I shall concentrate on making my own special mark on life in my own way.

Lord, we all want to
make a difference,
to leave a lasting mark
on this world.
Even when we live to
the same pattern,
life with you,
the marks we make
are all unique
and are all seen
and loved by you.
Thank you for those who
have made a mark
on my life.
Thank you for their time,
their care
and their love.
My own marks may not
change the world,
but Lord, help me today
to leave some
element of beauty behind.

Hanging from a cliff

Habakkuk 3:19
The Sovereign LORD is my strength; he makes my feet like the feet of a deer,
he enables me to tread on the heights.
(*New International Version*)

I am hanging from the cliff, the rope is tight and I am swinging from side to side trying not to look down and very aware of the massive climb to the top, as well as the drop below.

Well, actually, I am not literally hanging from a cliff at all, but it feels like it. And those of you who know me know I would never be anywhere near a real cliff, never mind hanging off the edge of one. I don't like heights. But it's a good picture for how I feel.

Life is hard at the moment, and I have had to face some painful truths that I have been hiding from up to now. When there are mountains to climb in my life, I am glad to remember the sturdy ropes that are preventing me from falling. It's what I sometimes refer to as my 'irreducible minimum.' My faith: *There is a God. Jesus died for me. I am redeemed and loved.* These are the essential facts that I cling to and that I know without a doubt.

These strong beliefs support me, especially when my theology looks greyer than usual. I have more questions than ever, but I have discovered that these ropes are strong and will not break. That comforts me. I can even laugh at myself, hanging there, worrying about stuff that is out of my control. I don't like heights at the best of times, but I can't run from life, so I will carry on and trust that my God is holding the ropes, and isn't about to let me go. And I know that if I stop struggling he will help me get to the very top of my imaginary cliff, to overcome my current difficulties and find peace.

Lord, I see the picture now.
Hanging from a high cliff,
wondering how I got here
and hoping I won't fall.
The ropes of my faith
are still intact.
Keeping me safe.
I see how strong they are
and it surprises me.
I know that I need to relax
and let you take my weight.
For I believe
You are God.
You died.
You rose,
and I am safe.
Thank you.

My head - the TARDIS

2 Corinthians 10:5

We demolish arguments and every pretension that sets itself up against the knowledge of God, and we take captive every thought to make it obedient to Christ.

(*New International Version*)

Mark Twain, the author of *Huckleberry Finn*, apparently once said "I have experienced many terrible things in my life, and some of them actually happened." I can so identify with him. I have always had a vivid imagination, as a child seeing shapes in the dark and looking under my bed for monsters, and now in my middle age still sometimes fearing things to come when there is little possibility of them actually happening.

If you ever watch *Doctor Who*, you will be familiar with the TARDIS. It's a black police call box that Doctor Who always arrives in. It's a normal-sized phone box on the outside, but inside, you discover a massive room totally out of proportion to the exterior size. It's full of stuff. Machines. Flashing lights. Levers and buttons that promise lift-off or disaster if you hit the wrong button. The inside of my head is like that. A huge space just waiting to fill up with stuff, some good, but often thoughts that do not belong there, vivid imaginings, doubts and worries, snapshots of potential disasters. I can get so absorbed with the details that I feel lost. Then, something outside of myself grabs my attention and I realise there is still a world out there, and all is well with it. Mark Twain's words help me to laugh at myself. Most of my worries will come to nothing and God wants to set us free from them, whether they are real or imagined.

I love the Bible verse above, it encourages us to take any rogue thought by the shoulders, shake it, tell it off, take it captive and make it obey God. And then there is my God, who can do so much more than my head can ever imagine. He is my true perspective. I need to step outside more often and see the real world through His eyes. And it's a great place to be today.

> Lord, I am so grateful for your reassurance. You know me. You understand what it's like inside my head. For you made me.
>
> Help us to take captive our doubts and worries and to rejoice in your promise, that there is so much more for us to enjoy.

A chicken and a chocolate cake

1 Peter 1:3
All praise to God, the Father of our Lord Jesus Christ. It is by his great mercy
that we have been born again, because God raised Jesus Christ from the dead.
Now we live with great expectation…

(*New Living Translation*)

I have a habit of leaving the best until last. The last mouthful of a meal, the nicest part of a cake… Years ago we were walking around Buttermere Lake in the Lake District. It's a gentle walk around the water's edge, nothing too taxing, and we had stopped, as we often do, to enjoy a flask of coffee and a cake. We know the Lake District well, but more especially, we know where all the nicest bakeries and tea shops are, so that we can buy enough cakes to keep us going on any long walk.

On this particular day, I had a large piece of chocolate cake to enjoy. We sat at the water's edge on a log, drinking our coffee, and eating. I had done my usual thing of eating the cake and leaving the two layers of chocolate icing until last. It's almost a family tradition. I can remember Dad's habit of eating the white of his fried egg first, working his way carefully around the yolk, and then downing the whole yolk as the last mouthful. I also remember my sister biding her time one day and then distracting him at the last minute so she could grab the precious yolk and eat it herself!

Anyway, I digress, I was just about to eat the icing when we noticed some chickens pecking in the leaves near our feet. I was admiring them when, suddenly, the largest bird, a brazen cockerel, launched itself at me and, before I could react, stole the icing out of my hand and ate it all.

I was, you might say, incandescent with rage. He had eaten my last mouthful, the 'best' bit of all, I had walked several miles looking forward to it and now I was left with an empty hand and a bad temper. Apart from being stunned at the discovery that chickens like chocolate, I think the moral of this story is… if you see chickens when you are eating cake, run in the opposite direction and perhaps don't leave the nicest things until last. The chicken, or even small children, might get there before you.

Seriously though, in life deciding to leave things until last doesn't always work. The opportunity may be gone before we know it and we are left wishing we had made a decision earlier. In Christian terms, the best Is yet to come, and it seems sad that some of us will put off making a decision to think about God, or to change our lives until a later date. If we do that, we will be missing out on enjoying the abundant life God gives to us in the here and now, and the opportunity to live by His spirit and experience His presence today.

> Lord, thank you that when we live our lives with you we know that the best is yet to come, the icing on the cake, the promised joy of heaven. But help us also to enjoy living in your presence now, walking and talking with You and including You in our everyday lives as we anticipate the joy of spending eternity with you.

Guerrilla knitting

Exodus 35:35
And he has given them all kinds of artistic skills, including the ability to design and embroider with blue, purple, and red wool and to weave fine linen.
(*Contemporary English Version*)

Be careful! There are guerrillas about and not the usual sort. You may see their work hanging from fences by the seaside, or on lamp posts in your high street. Wherever they are, seeing their work will at least make you stop and stare and, at best, make you laugh. It's all about knitting, and I believe the current phrase in use is 'you've been yarn-bombed.'

There are people all over the country meeting to knit scarves for lamp posts and flowers for fences with the sole idea of making people stop in the midst of their busy-ness, to pause and smile.

I have seen their work in Devon and Cornwall and on the high street in Kendal, Cumbria. The most recent ones in Kendal were little knitted dogs and cats fixed to lamp posts by scarves. Beautifully made and colourful on a grey day. I am reminded of the word 'grace-note'. It means 'an embellishment not essential to the harmony: an ornament.'

I love the idea of people getting together to make something that will grace and embellish our day-to-day lives. These things are neither essential nor life changing, but they do make a difference.

I'm not trying to spiritualize guerrilla knitting or any other form of creativity, but I like to think that God cares about the small stuff, and can inspire us to do creative things just for the fun of it. Anything that will encourage us to pause, see something out of the ordinary and smile has to be good.

Lord, I love people's creativity.
New ideas, however small,
carried through
to make us smile.
Adding to life,
a simple grace note;
it doesn't change the melody
but brings a beauty of its own.
Lord, bless those who
take the time,
those who see a space
to be filled
and make something lovely.
Help me to add something
beautiful too.

I've closed my eyes

Proverbs 20:12
Ears to hear and eyes to see – both are gifts from the LORD.
(New Living Translation)

I am a vegetarian, as is my lovely daughter, and my son is a vegan. My poor husband doesn't stand any chance of seeing much meat in our house these days. I try not to be too persuasive about it, although I'm beginning to think that maybe I should be.

Sometimes the vegetarian issue crops up when we are with friends, as it did the other day. My god-daughter Elly had been staying with us for a while and seemed to have enjoyed the vegetarian food we cooked.

Later, I asked her jokingly, "Have you seen the light yet?" I knew she had enjoyed a bacon butty on the train on her way back home, probably with a certain amount of relief. She laughed and said "Oh, I've seen the light, but I've closed my eyes."

An honest response and it made us laugh, but it did make me think, too. What have I seen lately and then closed my eyes to?

> Lord, teach me not to look away.
> You saw so much and never turned away from people's need.
> You held their gaze, and looked into their hearts, willing to see and listen, driven by love.
> Forgive our lack of care and let us see with your eyes today.
> Let us be your hands and feet, and speak out with your voice today.

We are bombarded by so much, and sometimes I find it easier to turn my head, and look away. We are exposed to so much through the television, newspapers and internet and at times I am tempted to turn away, to close my eyes. Turning my television off is easy, but the need is still there, waiting to be answered. Jesus wants us to be his voice, his hands and feet and sometimes I need to stop and ask God what he wants me to see today and what he wants me to do about it. I wonder, what would we do differently if we could see the world completely through God's eyes?

And by the way, Elly, if you are reading this, it's not too late to change your mind!

Water into wine

John 2:6

Nearby stood six stone water jars, the kind used by Jews for ceremonial washing, each holding twenty to thirty gallons.

(New International Version)

This is an interesting story, isn't it? I've often wondered why Jesus' first miracle involved wine. And there was a lot of it. Then I noticed something. In John chapter 2, we are told that the jars that Jesus told the servants to fill were ceremonial jars, used for the ritual of cleansing, signifying spiritual washing.

There is a wonderful irony here. Jesus is at a wedding, probably a noisy one, with guests on their way to being merry, if not drunk. A happy atmosphere. And then the worst happens. The wine runs out. Jesus steps in and helps out in a very practical way, but look at what he is using to hold the wine.

It's as if he is saying, 'Look, I am here now. I am the one who will make you clean, from the inside out. It will no longer be just a ritual cleansing but a lasting one. I am the better way. And I will provide the wine for you too.' I love that. I can almost see the smile on his face, waiting to see if anyone will realise the deeper significance.

And by the way, with six stone jars of that size, the quantity would be over 600 modern day bottles of wine at a conservative estimate. I'd love to have been there to see the look on the servants' faces as they saw what was happening.

Lord, I love what you do,
getting involved with our
everyday concerns
and then turning
them around.
Giving small things a much
deeper meaning.
I know I haven't seen
many miracles
yet,
but I read your words
and they change me.
Lord, would you open my eyes
to the everyday miracles
around me?

Don't just buy the tracksuit

Luke 8:13

The seeds that fell on rocky ground are the people who gladly hear the message and accept it. But they don't have deep roots, and they believe only for a little while. As soon as life gets hard, they give up.

(Contemporary English Version)

I had a patient a few years ago. I think he came to me for some physiotherapy for his back problem. As usual I would begin with a list of questions about his medical history, his job, hobbies etc. just to give me an idea of what his daily activities were in relation to his back. As it happened he wasn't really into any sport or aerobic training at all, so I encouraged him to think of something he might like to do to increase his fitness levels while he improved.

He came in the following month, very excited. He had bought an exercise bike the week after I had seen him and a tracksuit to go with it. I asked him how he was getting on with using it. He pretended to be surprised by my question, "Oh, I haven't actually used the tracksuit yet," he said with a grin, "but I have bought it, isn't that enough?" He clearly felt fitter just by buying the kit and dared to hope that would be enough! If only it were that easy. A great start, but it went no further. Somehow, the action itself never happened.

Lord, is this what you meant,
by the abundant life?
A life trusting in your goodness,
peppered with some risk taking,
seeing your kingdom come
into the world around me.
Lord, I've got my tracksuit on
today,
my trainers on my feet and I'm
ready to go.
I want this way of life
to be mine.
Train me, set my pace,
and let me run by your side today.

In the same way, it's easy for me to go and buy the paintbrushes, the art paper, the 'how to paint' books, but I have to get started to make a difference, to learn, and allow myself to make mistakes. It's easy to talk, to agree with the theory but, if I want to improve, I have to go into my summerhouse and start painting. I have to take the first step and put it into practice.

Our Christian faith is just the same. We are saved by grace, but the evidence of our faith is seen in our actions. We can go to church week by week, we can listen to the sermon and sing about Jesus, but unless we put it into practice, nothing in our lives will change. Perhaps I need to go out on the streets and pray for someone, help my neighbour with his garden, do someone's shopping or help at a local food bank. The possibilities are endless, and if I think about it in the right way, it looks an exciting way to live.

The fragrance of God

John 12:3

Then Mary took about half a litre of pure nard, an expensive perfume;
she poured it on Jesus' feet and wiped his feet with her hair.
And the house was filled with the fragrance of the perfume.

(New International Version)

I bought a T-shirt this week; it's a lovely petrol blue colour with a scoop neck. I wore it yesterday and suddenly noticed it had a small logo on the front of the left shoulder. It says 'G-sus'. It sounds like 'Jesus'. I'm pretty sure the company that made it didn't mean me to make that connection, but I like the idea of having a reminder of Jesus on my shoulder. It makes me think about what is important to me.

Lord, we can imagine the scene,
the room so full,
and then Mary appears.
The perfume is broken
and the air fills with the heavy
fragrance.
There it was,
a reminder of her overflowing love
for you.
Lord, let our own love for you
show.
Let it fill us like a fragrance
that we carry with us,
bringing a peace to others
that only You can give.

Years ago, in the early seventies, there was a craze for wearing 'Smile, Jesus loves you' stickers. Perhaps you remember them? They were bright orange and I wore them a lot. The only problem at the time was that I was going through my 'sulky teenager' phase and, whilst on holiday with my poor parents, I remember Dad quipping that I should either take the sticker off or learn to smile again. I didn't much appreciate it at the time, but he was right. And I did take the sticker off. And probably sulked some more.

The wonderful thing is that if we stay close to Jesus, there is a certain something about us that other people seem able to see, maybe in our eyes or in our smile, but they see a light there. It's as if we carry the fragrance of God with us. We don't need a sticker, or a logo, because Jesus will shine through us.

When Mary broke open the perfume, the room was filled with its fragrance, and there was no escaping it. I have met some Christians who seem to carry this fragrance in abundance. They fill the room with a certain peace and light that makes me unwilling to leave them. I can imagine that even after Mary

and all the others had gone home, the fragrance would have lingered in the room for days, as well as on the clothes of those who were there at the time. I long to have the same effect, so that the Holy Spirit in me will overflow onto others so they will feel God's love for them.

The revenge of a small dog

Our friend, Jon, has a small brown dog called Reggie who is under the
impression he is a big brown dog. He has what some people call 'small dog
syndrome'. He believes he is big, and no one can tell him otherwise. Now
Reggie hated our dog, Morty, on first sight because Morty is a big dog and
since that first meeting, Reggie barks aggressively at Morty every time he
sees him.

We were visiting them recently in the Lake District and that day we foolishly
decided to drive out to a favourite walk with both the dogs in the same car.
Morty was harnessed safely in the back seat next to me and initially Jon put
Reggie on his knee, but after five minutes of frenzied barking at Morty, he
was soundly told off and banished to the floor in disgrace.

All was quiet. Jon was praising Reggie for calming down and being so good, and we all wanted to believe that this heralded a new era. We stopped at the car park and heard Jon say in a worried voice, "What on earth is this?" He was holding what was once the input lead for an iPod that was now merely a handful of short chewed wires. Reggie was told off, but he probably didn't hear as I was laughing so loudly. No wonder he had been so quiet. The initial worry was whether Reggie had swallowed the entire plastic end of the wires and my mind immediately filled with possible horrible scenarios at the vet.

Worse was to come as Jon reached for Reggie's lead, which should have been attached to him. Only six inches of it remained, hanging soggily from his collar. Reggie remained impassive throughout. I was nearly hysterical by this time, my sides aching with laughing so much, and I was only vaguely aware of Jon trying to tell the dog off again, in a rather desperate attempt to save face and make it look like he was still in control.

We found the plastic end of the input lead, and we did manage the walk in the end, using a spare dog lead we had in the boot. Jon kept muttering something about Reggie behaving badly to get his revenge for having been told off the first time. I'm not sure if dogs think about revenge, but revenge in any situation is never a good thing. It only leads to more problems and, in this case, a further and even stronger telling off. My husband, Peter, thinks Reggie was waiting for his moment and I haven't laughed so much for a long while, so perhaps the two damaged leads were worth it. Although I'm not sure Jon would agree.

Lord, sometimes it's easy to
get angry,
to want revenge,
a payback for a wrong done to us.
Justice on our terms
for the unfairness of it all.
But you talked of a different way,
of letting go,
of forgiveness,
and love,
and the freedom to move on.
Lord, would you help us
to let go of grievances
to choose a better way,
your way.
And it's only by the help of your
spirit that we can.
Thank you.

Always friends

John 15:12–15

My command is this: Love each other as I have loved you. Greater love has no one than this: to lay down one's life for one's friends. You are my friends if you do what I command. I no longer call you servants, because a servant does not know his master's business. Instead, I have called you friends, for everything that I learned from my Father I have made known to you.

(New International Version)

We go walking every day with our hairy dog, Mortimer, in Nonsuch Park, which is local to us. It's a beautiful place with hundreds of trees and a lot of history behind it. It once formed part of one of Henry VIII's Great Parks. Up until The Great Storm of 1987, there were two great oaks that were reputed to date from that time but, sadly, they came down during the storm. I'm embarrassed to say we slept through the entire storm, even though a large tree came down outside our house, but that's another story entirely.

On this particular day, we were on the lookout as always for other dogs for Morty to play with, when we recognised a familiar black dog on the far edge of the field. It was Rosie, the wonderful large Briard who Morty has a special relationship with. After a rapturous welcome, we stood chatting with the owners while the dogs ran circles with their heads together and tails wagging. We hadn't seen Rosie for over five months. Our times in the park simply hadn't coincided with theirs but there they were, racing around like close friends. The canine connection was and is still very close.

And then it occurred to me. Human friendships can be like that too. We have very precious friends in the Lake District whom we have known for over thirty years. Actually, they are the owners of the infamous Reggie (see page 48). We travel to see them two or three times a year, and it is always the same the minute we walk in. It's as if we had only met a few days ago. No need for niceties, apologies or any strangeness between us.

Lord, thank you for close friends for they are an example of your love for me.
Always accepting, welcoming me with joy sharing their lives with me.
I see you in them.
Help me to see you in the same way, always there, ready to welcome me with your arms wide open.

We simply pick up where we left off, as the saying goes. It's a wonderful thing and we all treasure it.

I know God is like that, too. It's easy for me to assume that he might be angry with me if I have been absent from church, forgotten to pray or neglected to read my Bible, but in my heart I know that he delights in our contact. The moment I turn my attention to him, there is no strangeness on his part, only a warm welcome, instant acceptance and a feeling of overwhelming love.

Where's the cheese?

1 Samuel 16:7
But the LORD said to Samuel, "... The LORD does not look at the things people look at. People look at the outward appearance, but the Lord looks at the heart."
(*New International Version*)

Growing up in India meant we didn't have certain types of food, mainly treats that Mum and Dad missed. Things like marmalade, *Marmite*, chocolate, and cheese. We always had plenty of food and, to be honest, I always preferred curry to a stew, but Mum especially found it hard.

Our lovely grandmother would send out food parcels to us every now and again. I can remember the excitement when Dad brought the parcel home from the office. As a child, I was always hoping Grandma would have sent my favourite thing, Licorice Allsorts. And this time she had. I don't remember what my sister, Stephanie, received but the best thing for Dad was a large piece of Stilton cheese.

In those days, the parcel had to travel by ship, and then overland by train so I hate to think of the resulting smell, but Dad took the cheese and put it safely into the pantry anyway. A day later and we were sitting at the dining table when Dad decided he would like to try some of the Stilton and went to look for it. When he couldn't find it he called for our cook, Jeshua, and asked him where it was.

Jeshua answered quickly, "Oh Sahib, the cheese was mouldy, so I threw it away." Dad was speechless. That piece of cheese had travelled over 4,000 miles by sea and train only to be consigned to the bin. Dad hadn't eaten proper cheese for a year. And Jeshua seemed horrified to think we might have been contemplating eating something that was covered in mould. Poor Dad, he got over it in time, but I don't remember another piece of cheese ever being sent out from England.

Every culture has its different traditions, and Jeshua thought he was doing the right thing. The idea of eating something so mouldy was a horrible idea to him. He took one look at the outward appearance and immediately judged the cheese to be unhealthy.

I wonder if we do the same without realising it, judging people and traditions by outward appearances, too readily dismissing something, or someone, without taking the time to understand.

Lord, I find it too easy to make up my mind about people and circumstances, forming opinions that I find hard to shake.
You see so clearly, seeing the heart of the person and not judging by actions alone.
Please give me that space to pause and see with your eyes, so my understanding is flavoured with your love.

The storm family

Psalm 107: 29

He stilled the storm to a whisper; the waves of the sea were hushed.

(*New International Version*)

If you haven't heard of Garrison Keillor then do look him up. He is an author, composer, singer and storyteller. You might have heard his 'Lake Woebegone' series which he read on Radio 4 many years ago. It was, I think, based on his American childhood. Do listen to the stories, if you can. His voice has a wonderful gravelly drawl to it and he is a master of understatement.

One particular story highlighted the fact that children who lived in a rural community in America often had to travel some miles to attend school. During the hurricane season, there wasn't always time to get back home so each child was given a 'storm family' who were situated in the town where they could take shelter when the hurricanes came – a special place to run to, a refuge.

I really like the idea of having my own storm family, a friend or a group of friends who will help me in times of crisis. Our families aren't always geographically close to us so perhaps we all need a 'storm family', a place where we can go for support when times are hard.

I know who my storm family is, and I like to think I can provide a refuge from the storm for little Grace and her family. Ultimately, Jesus is the best sanctuary for believers, but sometimes we also need a physical pair of arms to hold onto us until the crisis is past.

Look around you and see who might need you to be a 'storm friend'. It's a privileged position to be in. And make sure you know who your 'storm family and friends' are. You may well need them and they in turn might need you.

Lord, you remind us often that
you are our refuge,
our high tower,
a safe place in any storm,
but often I forget to run to you,
so caught up in the immediacy of
my needs
I seem paralysed and lose my way.
Call me, Lord,
when times get tough,
and lead me to safety,
for you are my shelter from
any storm.
Keep your arms around me
until the strong winds have passed
and I can hear again
your still small voice of calm.

Turning upside down!

1 Peter 5:7
Cast all your anxiety on him because he cares for you.
(*New International Version*)

I found a wonderful card some months ago. I was looking for something to cheer up a friend who had been quite sick. The picture was a lovely photo of a young child on the floor with her legs over her head, and the special quote from Jack, age 6, made me laugh out loud.

'Turning upside down makes you happy because the sad feelings get all dizzy and fall out.'

The innocence mixed with the curious child-like logic is so appealing. I have tried to do the same, put my legs over my head that is, though laughing in that position can be a little dangerous and I can hear a government health warning in the background, so please don't try it at home! But it's a great thought, isn't it? Every time you feel sad or troubled, simply turn upside down to feel better. Let the sad feelings just tumble out.

Sadly, life isn't that simple, or is it? Many verses in the Bible are about dealing with our feelings. Jesus knew what it was like to be fully human, to feel fear, sadness, frustration and anger. He tells us to take our feelings straight to him and not to worry. It sounds as easy as letting them tumble out of our heads, but in practice, it's a bit harder. Maybe we need to be in the right position to do it, staying close to Him and following what He says. And that's something we can try safely at home!

Lord, I know I need to lighten up sometimes
and not take myself so seriously.
Try a little laughter.
Do something different.
A bit like standing on my head.
My perspective on life will change
and I might feel better.
Even if I can't physically get into that position,
I can ask for your help
and let the sad feelings
tumble away.